The Curies
and Radioactivity

Yoming S. Lin

PowerKiDS press.

New York

To my dear friends, Emily and Irene

Published in 2012 by The Rosen Publishing Group, Inc.
29 East 21st Street, New York, NY 10010

First Edition

Editor: Amelie von Zumbusch
Book Design: Greg Tucker

Photo Credits: Cover (main), p. 20 (top left) Agence France-Presse/Getty Images; cover (rock), pp. 5 (bottom), 7 (bottom), 9 (top, bottom), 13, 17 (bottom), 19 (top), 20 (bottom), 21 (bottom) Shutterstock.com; p. 4 Library of Congress/digital version by Science Faction/Getty Images; pp. 5 (top), 19 (bottom) Apic/Getty Images; pp. 6, 7 (top), 8, 12, 17 (top), 18 Photos.com/Thinkstock; p. 10 AFP/Getty Images; p. 11 (top) Branger/Roger Viollet/Getty Images; p. 11 (bottom) © www.iStockphoto.com/peterspiro; pp. 14–15 Fox Photos/Getty Images; p. 16 Time & Life Pictures/Mansell/Getty Images; p. 20 (top right) Science and Society Picture Library/Getty Images; p. 21 (top) U.S. Army Signal Corps/Time & Life Pictures/Getty Images.

Library of Congress Cataloging-in-Publication Data

Lin, Yoming S.
  The Curies and radioactivity / by Yoming S. Lin. — 1st ed.
      p. cm. — (Eureka!)
  Includes index.
  ISBN 978-1-4488-5033-4 (library binding)
  1. Curie, Marie, 1867-1934—Juvenile literature. 2. Curie, Pierre, 1859-1906—Juvenile literature. 3. Chemists—Poland—Biography—Juvenile literature. 4. Chemists—France—Biography—Juvenile literature. 5. Radioactivity—History—Juvenile literature. I. Title.
  QD22.C8L56 2012
  540.92'244—dc22
  [B]
                                    2011004400

Manufactured in the United States of America

CPSIA Compliance Information: Batch #WS11PK: For Further Information contact Rosen Publishing, New York, New York at 1-800-237-9932

Contents

Two Great Scientists

Pierre and Marie Curie were two scientists born in the middle of the nineteenth century. They were partners in marriage and in work. Pierre and Marie Curie were hardworking, smart, and had similar interests. They worked very well together. They

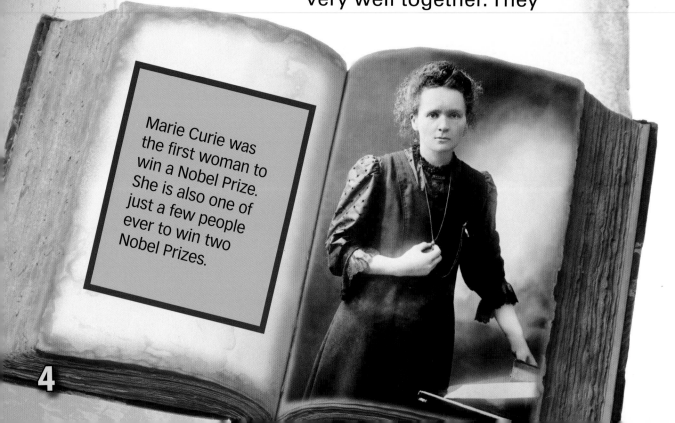

Marie Curie was the first woman to win a Nobel Prize. She is also one of just a few people ever to win two Nobel Prizes.

teamed up to make big discoveries.

They were awarded the Nobel Prize, a great honor, for their work on radioactivity. Some types of **matter**, or things, give off rays of energy. This is called radioactivity. The Curies' work on radioactivity made them famous. It also helped scientists better understand the nature of matter. It is the basis of many important scientific developments that have changed the world.

Top: Pierre Curie was more interested in doing science experiments than in becoming a famous scientist. *Bottom*: Radioactive matter is often marked with signs like this one.

RADIOACTIVE

Marie Skłodowska was born in 1867 in Warsaw, Poland. She had three sisters and one brother. Her parents, Bronisława and Władysław, were teachers. At that time, Russia controlled Warsaw and other parts of Poland. Many Polish people were unhappy about this. Marie's parents spoke against Russian rule and got

Marie (left) worked as a governess, or private teacher, to help Bronya (right) pay for her education as a doctor. Bronya later helped pay for Marie's studies.

in trouble. This forced Władysław to take jobs that paid poorly. The family faced hard times. Marie's oldest sister died when Marie was eight. Their mother died a few years later.

Marie's family was close. Their father read to the children and taught them about science. Marie was a good student. After high school, Marie worked to pay for her sister Bronya's studies.

Top: Here Marie is with her brother and her sisters. She is seated, at right. *Bottom*: Warsaw has long been Poland's biggest city. Today it is the capital, too.

Pierre Curie was born in 1859 in Paris, France. Pierre was smart. His father, Eugène, hired private teachers for him. Pierre then studied at the Sorbonne, a university in Paris. He graduated from the Sorbonne at 18. He wanted to study for a **doctorate**, the highest level of schooling in science. He did not have the money, though.

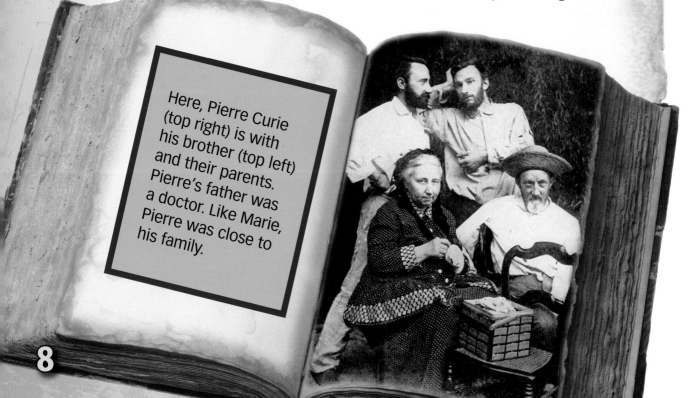

Here, Pierre Curie (top right) is with his brother (top left) and their parents. Pierre's father was a doctor. Like Marie, Pierre was close to his family.

When Pierre was 21 years old, he and his brother, Jacques, discovered something interesting about **crystals**. Crystals are matter with fixed shapes. The brothers saw that electricity flows out of certain crystals when they are pressed on. When these crystals are placed near electricity, they get smaller. They used this knowledge to invent a kind of **electrometer**. It used crystals to measure electric **currents**.

Top: Quartz crystals make a flow of electricity when pressed on. *Bottom*: Many modern machines, such as computers, depend on the way certain crystals act when pressed on.

9

In 1891, Marie went to Paris to study at the Sorbonne. At first, she fell behind her classmates because she found that she was not as prepared as them. She worked hard, though, and ended up graduating first in her **physics** class! Physics is the study of energy and matter. A year later, she

Marie and Pierre had many of the same interests. They worked well together and were big backers of each other's work.

graduated second among the math students.

After that, she looked for a lab where she could work. She ended up working in a small space at Pierre Curie's lab. They got along well and fell in love. Marie and Pierre married in 1895. They would have two daughters together. The Curies had very little money but were a happy couple.

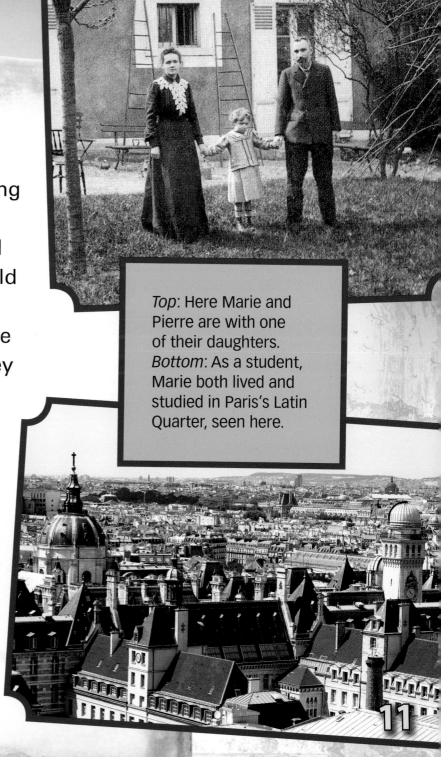

Top: Here Marie and Pierre are with one of their daughters. *Bottom*: As a student, Marie both lived and studied in Paris's Latin Quarter, seen here.

The Curies both decided to get their doctorates. Pierre did experiments with magnets. He discovered that how hot a magnet is can change how strong its pull is.

In the mid-1890s, Marie learned about the discoveries of two scientists. Wilhelm Roentgen had discovered the **X-ray**. This kind of ray could travel through flesh and be used to take pictures of people's

Henri Becquerel was born and spent his life in Paris. Becquerel came from a family of scientists. He studied many things, including magnets and light.

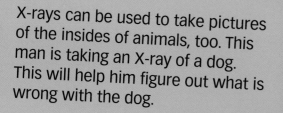

X-rays can be used to take pictures of the insides of animals, too. This man is taking an X-ray of a dog. This will help him figure out what is wrong with the dog.

bones. In 1896, Henri Becquerel had noticed that the **element** uranium **emits**, or gives off, rays. An element is one of the basic kinds of matter. Uranium's rays were strong enough to make a foggy picture on a photo. Marie decided to study the rays for her doctorate.

Radioactivity

Marie knew that all matter is made of tiny parts called **atoms**. Atoms can be arranged in different ways. Marie found that how many rays uranium emitted was not tied to how its atoms were arranged. Only the amount of uranium changed the rays' strength. She guessed that this meant that something inside the atoms produced the rays.

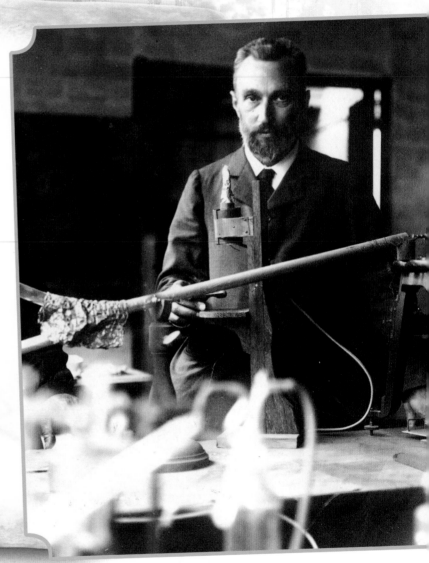

Here, Pierre and Marie Curie are at work in their lab. Marie was the first person to call the rays emitted by certain elements radioactivity.

Marie found that the element thorium emitted rays like those of uranium. Electric currents were present near these rays. The more rays there were, the stronger the currents were. The Curies separated out the matter that emitted the strongest rays with an electrometer. They discovered two new elements, which they named radium and polonium.

In 1903, Marie and Pierre won the Nobel Prize in Physics for their work on radioactivity. They shared the prize with Henri Becquerel. That same year, Marie became the first woman in France to get a doctorate.

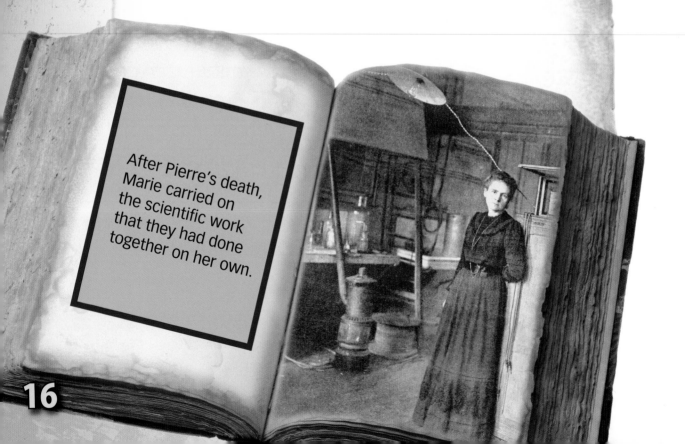

After Pierre's death, Marie carried on the scientific work that they had done together on her own.

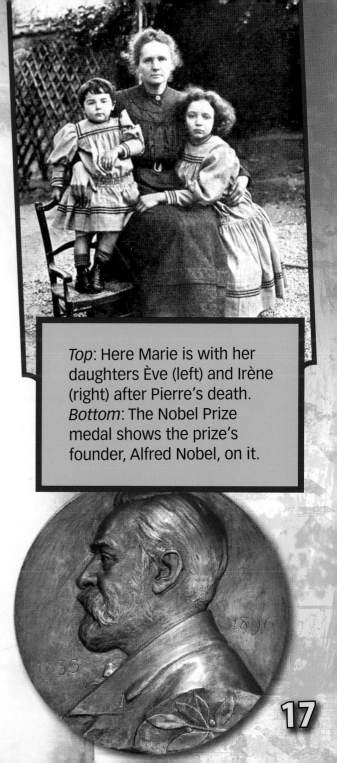

In 1906, Pierre died after being hit by a carriage while crossing the street. Marie was very sad. The Sorbonne asked her to take over Pierre's job as a **professor**, or teacher, there. She became the Sorbonne's first female professor. Marie also started a lab to honor Pierre's memory.

In 1911, Marie won the Nobel Prize in **Chemistry**, or the study of matter. The award was for discovering new elements and separating out a sample of radium.

Top: Here Marie is with her daughters Ève (left) and Irène (right) after Pierre's death. *Bottom*: The Nobel Prize medal shows the prize's founder, Alfred Nobel, on it.

17

In 1914, World War I broke out in Europe. Marie set up X-ray centers to treat wounded French soldiers. After the war, she worked for the Radium Institute, a new scientific center.

Marie also studied how radioactivity could be used in medicine. Pierre had rightly guessed that radium could be

Some of the X-ray centers Marie set up to treat soldiers in World War I were in vans. These were known as *petite Curies*. Here she is driving one of them.

used to treat **cancer**, a sickness. Scientists would learn later that too much radioactivity could also cause cancer. In fact, being around radioactivity too much gave Marie cancer. She died of it in 1934.

Marie and Pierre's work changed science forever. Radioactivity is the basis of some of the ways doctors treat cancer today. The Curies' work has helped save many lives.

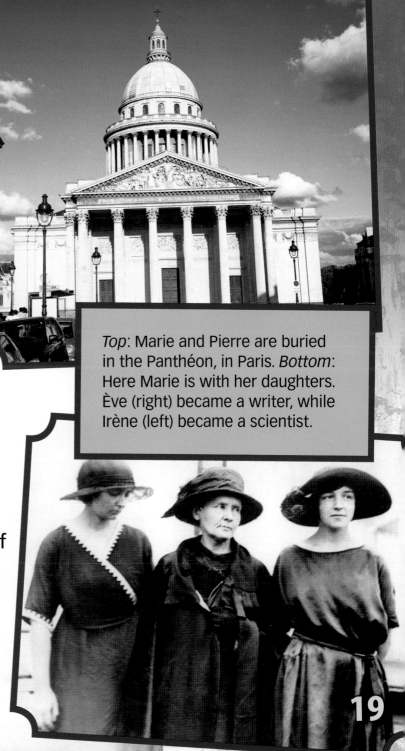

Top: Marie and Pierre are buried in the Panthéon, in Paris. *Bottom*: Here Marie is with her daughters. Ève (right) became a writer, while Irène (left) became a scientist.

Timeline

January 1863

The Polish rise against the Russians, who ruled parts of Poland. The Polish fight hard but do not succeed in getting rid of Russian rule.

1880

Pierre and his brother, Jacques, invent what became known as the Curie electrometer.

May 15, 1859

Pierre Curie is born in Paris, France, to Sophie-Claire and Eugène Curie.

1840   1850   1860   1870   1880   1890

November 7, 1867

Maria Skłodowska is born in Warsaw, Poland. She will later go by Marie, the French form of her name.

Summer 1893

Marie graduates first in her class for her degree in physics from the Sorbonne.

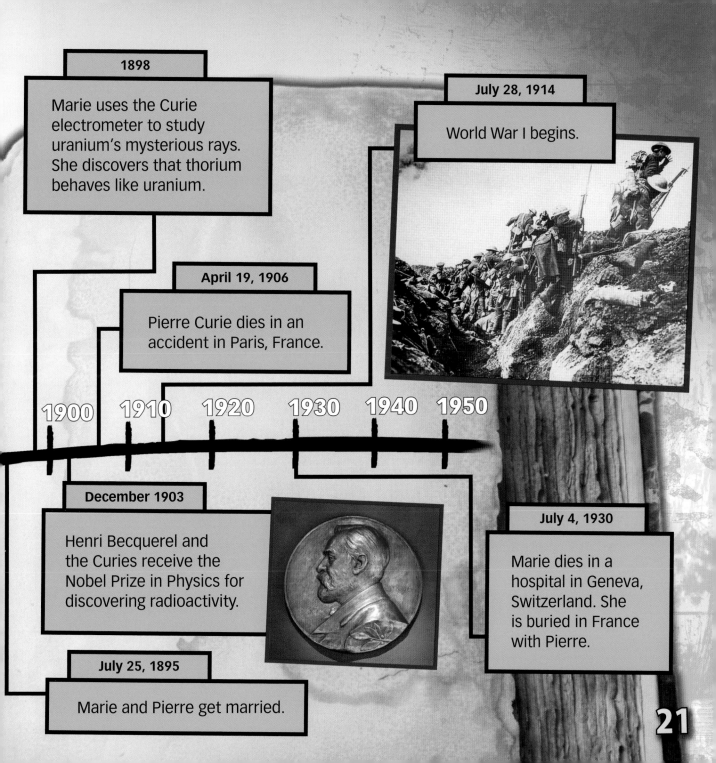

1898

Marie uses the Curie electrometer to study uranium's mysterious rays. She discovers that thorium behaves like uranium.

July 28, 1914

World War I begins.

April 19, 1906

Pierre Curie dies in an accident in Paris, France.

1900 1910 1920 1930 1940 1950

December 1903

Henri Becquerel and the Curies receive the Nobel Prize in Physics for discovering radioactivity.

July 4, 1930

Marie dies in a hospital in Geneva, Switzerland. She is buried in France with Pierre.

July 25, 1895

Marie and Pierre get married.

21

Inside the Science

1. When you take an X-ray, the rays go through skin and flesh and darken the X-ray film. The rays do not go through bones, though. This makes the bones look white in the picture. Doctors often use X-rays to look at broken bones.

2. Today, there are more than 100 different elements known to scientists. Curium is an element named in honor of the Curies.

3. Atoms are made of different parts. One of the parts is called a **proton**. Atoms of a certain element all have the same number of protons. If an element's number of protons changes, it becomes a different element.

4. Other scientists built on Marie Curie's work and studied the radioactive rays. They realized that some of the rays from the radioactive elements were streams of very small pieces of matter. They were not real rays at all!

5. Radioactivity can hurt people's bodies. Its rays can cause burns. They can hurt cells, or the parts that make up living things. Radioactivity can make cells grow out of control. This causes cancer.

Glossary

atoms (A-temz) The smallest parts of elements.

cancer (KAN-ser) A sickness in which cells multiply out of control and do not work the way they should.

chemistry (KEH-mih-stree) A type of science that deals with the way matter changes.

crystals (KRIS-tulz) Matter with an ordered pattern of atoms.

currents (KUR-ents) Flows of things in one direction.

doctorate (DOK-tuh-rut) The highest level of study in many fields.

electrometer (ih-lek-TRO-meh-ter) A tool that measures electricity.

element (EH-luh-ment) One of the basic kinds of matter of which all things are made.

emits (ee-MITS) Puts out.

matter (MA-ter) Anything that has weight and takes up space.

physics (FIH-ziks) The scientific study of matter and energy and their relationships to each other.

professor (preh-FEH-ser) A teacher at a college, or a school for advanced students.

proton (PROH-ton) A particle with a positive electric charge found in the nucleus of an atom.

X-ray (EKS-ray) A ray that can pass through matter that light rays cannot.

Index

Web Sites

Due to the changing nature of Internet links, PowerKids Press has developed an online list of Web sites related to the subject of this book. This site is updated regularly. Please use this link to access the list:
www.powerkidslinks.com/eure/curies/